A Multi-Approach to Understanding Human Existence

Sola Oloruada

A Multi-Approach

To

Understanding

Human Existence

By

Sola Olorunda

Sola Olorunda

Sola Olorunda Publishers

105 Farayola Street, Bodija Ibadan, Oyo State, Nigeria,

solaolorunda@gmail.com

+234 (0) 8038476260, +234 (0) 8024144440

Facebook: Sola Olorunda

Twitter: @sola_olorunda

Instagram: solaolorunda

Skype: Sola Olorunda

DEDICATION

This write-up is dedicated to the only supernatural power, who controls the universe, whom I regard as the positive thinking of human endeavour, Almighty God, and all the orphans in the society at large.

Table of Contents

FOREWORD

Whenever a young person exhibits certain unusual but positive talents in any society, he/she must be encouraged to actualize his dreams and potentials. Catch 'em young is a slogan that is yet to be fully practicalized in Nigeria. This lapse has invariably led to wastage of talents in academics, sports, drama, creative writing and other endeavors of human existence.

A young writer like Sola Oloruunda deserves societal encouragement as he ventures into the world of creative and imaginative writing. His debut, A MULTI-APPROACH TO UNDERSTANDING HUMAN EXISTENCE is a conglomerate of past and contemporary issues.

He agrees with a widely accepted notion that Man possesses extraordinary powers for good and for evil. Like many peace-loving humans across the globe, Sola is apprehensive that human existence faces possible extermination in the exploits of the human beast. The human beast whether as nuclear physicist or chemical engineer or biological weapon expert continues to invent new and increasingly deadly weapons of Mutually Assured Destruction (M.A.D)

The book devotes a large space to the alienation of nature by man and the irreversible consequences of environmental pollution. It also examines the origin and nature of man from three theories, viz the scientific, the Religious and the Mythical.

In fact the book is targeted at a wide audience as it focuses on a range of interrelated issues such as Education, Science and Technology, Socialization, Majority-Minority Relationships,

Inordinate Ambition, Secret Cults, Centres of Religious worship, Time Factor etc.

In the hope that Nigeria's reading public, especially the youth will free themselves from the shackles of over indulgence in watching films and video on the television. Sola's book is highly recommended for its insight and deep burrowing into certain fundamental issues of human existence. Obviously he was inspired and he too wants to inspire others.

Dr. Ademola Adeyanju

Head of Department of Curriculum and Instruction, Oyo State College of Education, Oyo. June, 2006.

INTRODUCTION

It is good to think of the workmanship of God which is marvelous. He has made us as wonderfully complex, even from the womb as we were being formed in utter seclusion, before our first breadth commenced. We need to appreciate God for giving us nature. In as much as this has been given to us, we need necessary compendiums and guidance to aid our civilization in this modern society.

To overcome these overwhelming strata of knowledge in society we need is **Independent Thinking,** It is the best policy in people's life. A problem is a chance for you to do your best. A MULTI-APPROACH TO UNDERSTANDING HUMAN EXISTENCE is a big revelation of issues in modern society.

You can preach a better sermon with your life than with your lips. The work of most leading philosophers in the previous era are unquestionable, they want us to understand the world at large better, they preached, encouraged and strengthened our beliefs and faith by their life time. But now our civilization has been able to realize that they were all seekers of knowledge, what they did at that time were not really compatible with our own modern societies, and most of their works are creative writing and drama.

What they emphasized was faith and to say the fact, faith wants us to believe, if you have faith you will believe and accept illusion as reality. In the previous era, what they packaged for us to believe, there would be positive and negative which we need to accept and reject as the world move forward because it is limited to their own olden days.

In the modern societies, a lot of research has been carried out in various fields of studies for the purpose of reducing human problems on earth. Government and private organizations have tried their best on poverty alleviation but all their efforts is not enough to reduce the forces of poverty in the society at large.

I believe this write-up will be useful for proper orientation and enlightenment of people concerning this predicament. Owing to the fact that our psychological problem cannot be solved by regression and our civilization is capable of redressing our modern society, I do not think we need to wait for anybody before we can re-order our modern society.

The works of Laymen and experts in the last century were enough for us to know that age are numbers. They did not neglect nature; they moved closer to it and brought something tangible out of it. Also, the works of such leading philosophers in the previous era are now revealed to us as abstract thoughts.

Goals are dreams we convert to plans and take action to fulfill. The main objective of this dream is to create awareness for modern people and proper orientation that will bridge the gap between people and nature. It is also aimed at stopping discrimination among the races in the world, this will enable individuals to develop their own 3Rs which is **(Respond to Realize Rescue).** This calls for total freedom from social bondage, because awareness removes ignorance, and in people's life every condition involves response. Finally history has where it locates itself, *"when you find a dream inside your heart, do not ever let it go, for dreams are seeds for a beautiful tomorrow"*

In conclusion, the law is a lamp, teaching is light and reproofs of instruction are the way of life. Everybody should know that "The rung of a ladder was never meant to be rested upon, but only to hold people's foot long enough to enable them to put the other somewhat higher".

Sola Olorunda (2006)

CHAPTER ONE

<u>WHO AM I?</u>

I had a dream. In this dream I thought of so many things of this life, especially the present condition of this society at large. I thought of the problems we are facing because life is so nasty and brutal for many people on earth. As I was thinking I sat under a big tree, when I looked up, I saw an old man walking towards me. When he got to my side, he said, my son, why are you sitting down here alone? I said I am exhausted by the countless problems of this particular place people called earth.

The old man said nothing should be tagged as a **Problem** because there is a solution to every occurrence on earth. He continued, perhaps, never before in history has people been so much problem to themselves, you have reached a point in history where knowledge and power intended originally to serve people now threaten to destroy them. What kind of society is this that loses control over its own power and creation? Your societies are in a state of flux, alienation is the central problem of your time, your society at large is rapidly becoming detached from nature, from their old gods.

From the technology that has transformed their environment and now threatens to destroy it, from their work and their products and from their leisure from the complex social institutions that presumably serve but are more likely to manipulate them, from the community in which they lives: and above all from themselves and from their body and their sex, from their feelings of love and tenderness and from their art, their creative and productive potentials.

I asked Him what alienation is and how people is alienated. He said the alienated person is everyone and anybody drifting in a world that has little meaning for them and over which they exercises no power, a stranger to themselves and to others. Alienation pervades the relationship of people to their work, to the things they consumes, to their fellows and to themselves, above all is that people have been separated from whatever might give meaning to their work and their lives.

By your modern term, however alienation has been used by philosophers, psychologists and sociologist to refer to an extraordinary variety of psycho-social disorder, including loss of self, anxiety, states, social disorganization, loneliness, powerlessness, meaninglessness, isolation and the loss of beliefs or values. Among the social groups who have been described as alienated in varying degrees are women, industrial workers, white collar workers, migrant workers, artists, suicides, the mentally disturbed, the aged, the young generation as a whole, juvenile delinquents in particular voters, non-voters, consumers, the audience of mass media, sex deviants, victims of prejudice and discrimination, the prejudiced, the bureaucrats, political radicals, the physically handicapped, immigrants, exiles, vagabonds and recluses.

Obviously you are dealing with a word that lends itself to many different meaning. He said the problems of selfhood has metaphysical or more properly ontological ramifications.

Alienation defined as loss of identity is better illustrated by men and women troubled over the simple yet complex question, **who am I?** The alienated people are the people who does not experience themselves as the center of their world, as the creator of their own acts- and their consequences have become their masters whom they obey or whom they may even worship. The alienated people are out of touch with themselves as they are out of touch with any other person.

Your society now-a-days is essentially violent in character: war, class struggles, hysterical crowd behaviour, vice and crime, plagues, scarcity, superstition, the conviction that the world was coming to an end and the long awaited second coming of the ego, such as the expectation of your generations which had been causing anxiety in your modern society.

But a stupid person will become wise when a wild donkey gives birth to human being. What you do not know that I must confess to all nations of the world and the society at large irrespective of race, ethnicity, religion affiliation and culture; to exist one had to belong to an association; a house-hold; a manor; a monastery; a guild. There was no security except in association and no freedom that did not recognize the obligation of a corporate life.

To say the fact, one lived and died in the style of one's class and corporation.

I asked this old man that was talking to me, why are the times so dark? People know each other not at all, but government quite clearly changed from bad to worse and also justice and law are nowhere to be found. He moved further with what you have just mentioned, in this case people must learn how to cope with countless problems and decisions that were once taken care of by worldly and spiritual hierarchies.

He said human achievement is a dialectical process in which people can advance to higher forms only by overcoming or mastering themselves and the cultural forces that they created. Therefore, the history of people is a history of their alienation or frustration, and of their self-realization through the conquest of these frustrations most people never experience the joys of a life plan, because most work situation do not afford the necessary stable progression over the work life. Civilization which brings about the science and technology had already depersonalized people themselves so effectively that they are no longer human enough to stand up to their machines, looking ahead the perfection of the automation, man will become completely alienated from their world and reduced to nullity because the kingdom, the power and the glory now belong to the machine.

People surrounded by things of whose nature and origin they know nothing about, lost where the customs and skills that had been passed on from one generation to another. Gone were the close bonds between young and old, and especially the respect that youth had previously given to the aged. Into the new industrial cities poured millions who had been cut off from the traditional family roots. Let me tell you, the deepest problems of your society nowadays are derived from the claim of the individual to preserve the autonomy and individuality of their existence in the face of overwhelming social forces. These pressures have mounted and people find it difficult to preserve their identity.

Science had been discovered which put the laws governing people's world beyond any doubt. It was at these laws that compassion was removed from the hearts and a stoic determination to renounce human solidarity in the name of the greatest happiness of the greatest number gained the dignity of religion. In a heterogeneous society like yours, there are numerous and sometimes overlapping minorities, yours is a multi-racial and multi-ethnic population. You need to think of such group in terms of colour and religious affiliation since these distinctions are among the most powerful of all social barriers.

Although, these sub-cultures offer some security and protection, common to most of them is a striving for integration with the majority groups on top. Furthermore, it is only natural for minority members to acquire some of the prevailing attitudes towards them, when this becomes self-hatred for sharing the despised characteristic; you have the most extreme from which this pattern of alienation takes: alienated from one another, they become alienated from themselves. What I mean was that men and women today are estranged from others as well as from themselves. But others mean not only the communities in which they live; it also refers to the natural and supernatural world beyond.

Thus if I speak of people's alienation from nature, I do not mean nature in any metaphysical sense, although fairly serious metaphysical problems are involved, all I mean is that men and women nowadays are not as close to land, air, sea, wind; and mountain as their ancestors who were not blessed with industrial and urban civilization deed.

To say the fact, the world is too much with you, why are you wasting your powers? The little you see in nature that is yours. It seems to me that people and nature were considered related parts of more or less harmonious whole, whether nature was considered hostile or friendly, people felt close to it. To understand and control the nature, the goals of modern science and technology, people first have to separate or alienate themselves from it, what were the consequence of this division between nature and people? First of all, it led to what I can now call the scientific attitude, as science develops it became more abstract and increasingly remote from common life. Science is the view of life where everything human is excluded from the prospect. It may be strange to you, but the further you travel from yourselves the nearer you approach the truth, for all you care for, the nearer you are to reality, the stony heart of the scientific universe.

The flowering of science and technology gave people enormous power to control nature and there by transform society. The language I used offers a clue to the new relationship between man and nature.

Thus when you speak of your power over nature you reveal a certain antagonism between man and external world, with nature regarded as something to be conquered or even destroyed. The greater that power, the more you are alienated from nature and from yourselves. The damage has already been done, the technology that classical science produced has erected almost insurmountable barriers between nature and people, the natural world.

Nature as people has always known it nowadays, they know no more, something is missing from your lives, are you not poorer for it? Isolation from nature is not just a matter of living in cities, people do not simply co-exist with nature, and they also search for meaning in it, for this they become dependent on myth and religion.

All religious beliefs known to people help to create and sustain bonds between them and the external world of other people and of nature, but if the faith weakens, or it is destroyed by onslaught of science and secularism, people are truly alone. The problem of mankind today is the opposite to that of people in the comparatively stable periods of those great coordinating mythologies which now are seen as lies. All meaning was in the group, in the great anonymous forms, none in the self-expressive individual. *Today, there is no meaning in the group, none in the world, all is in the individual. But one does not know toward what one moves, one does not know by what one is propelled, not the animal world, not the plant world, not the miracle of the spheres, but people themselves are now a crucial mystery.*

People's alienation began with whom the forces of egoism must come to terms, through with whom the ego is to be crucified and resurrected and whose image of society is to be reformed. A liberating process has also taken place and spiritual isolation is part of the price paid for new-found knowledge and power. The loss of religion may mean less psychological security but it has also meant more since it is accompanied, a great social and economic revolution. Society in its attack against the power, dogma, and the ritual of the universal religion helped to free people for worldly activities. People should learn how to face God alone without the intervention of any religion and stressed the fundamental evil and powerlessness of people, a great price was paid for that freedom.

Today, you live in an increasingly secularized society and religious faith is less than motivating force and an explanation of the world around you. Your culture is perhaps the first completely secularized culture in human history, you have shoved away awareness of and concern with the fundamental problems of human existence, and you are not concerned with the meaning of life.

Your society now-days is witnessing a revival, in which churches of all denomination resemble social clubs, and religion itself is secularized, it is very obvious that the religiousness with almost any kind of content or none, *where centers of religious worship now become invisible pawn, a way of sociability or belonging rather than a way of re-orienting to God.* It is thus frequently a religiousness without serious commitment, without real inner conviction, without genuine existential decision. Religious thus become a kind of protection, the self throws up against the radical demand of faith if so, is the weakening of traditional faith and the apparent search for a social rather than a spiritual community in the church or mosque, simply another measure of alienation? You now have a view of man divorced from nature, deprived of his religion, isolated in his community and chained to monotonous work. If many are persuaded to accept the spurious values handed down to them by religion, the society debases, it debases the state, man, woman, love, race, child, family and nation. It even has succeeded in debasing what is perhaps most difficult in the world to debase, because, this is something which has in itself, as in its texture a particular kind of dignity like a singular incapacity for degradation, it debases death.

The old man explained further, he said in another terms, alienation as an unwillingness to accept what the culture offers. The sharp knife of changing society has cut off all the threads by which in former generations, the state was fastened to the organic whole of human existence. The political world has lost its connection not only with religion or metaphysics but also with all the other forms of people ethical and cultural life. It stands alone in an empty space. In democratic societies also government, like so many other social institution originally designed to serve people has threatens to become their master, I must tell you that the traditional primary relationship of people has become functionally irrelevant to your state and economy and meaningless to the moral aspiration of individuals. The state has power to do great good as well as evil and you are not joining those true reactionaries who dream of dismantling it. What I was suggesting is that the nation even when providing necessary services is detached from individual needs. How to redress this imbalance between state and people has become a burning issues for all people right and left, and I asked the old man, who would re-order our society. He said *over-civilization and accompanying dehumanization are the most crucial problems of your society,* let me differentiate your present malady from those of old days in terms of the void between hopes and reality. In the course of history, alienation has undergone significant qualitative changes so that its meaning today is quite different from what it was in previous eras. In the present stage of history, people has means of self-realization at their command which were unknown to them in former periods. The immense advances of science and technology has helped them to understand the forces of nature to such a degree that it is no longer at their mercy. It has become their master and has succeeded in subjecting them to its ends with this tremendous progress toward the realization of the promenade dream , a new image has arisen of people who shapes their life and it is master of their destiny.

Once this concept of the individual's sovereignty has been awakened in the minds of people, a new climate was prepared. The consciousness that people's strong emotional desire for self-realization is thwarted becomes a crushing experience which could not have existed in previous stages. In such a situation the alienation of people is no longer accepted as an inevitable fate; more than ever before in history, it is felt as a threat and at the same time a challenge. I asked him, how people should face this challenge? And I think of personality changes to minor reforms which would have intact the basic social and economic structure, thus more faith is called for, or more humor, more housing, more food, more material comforts, more education to improve people's lot, but if that fails more philosophy to endure and somehow find fragmentary enjoyment in pleasures, also let us return to religion and sharp awareness of the possibly utilitarian value of prayer and believe in the power of " **positive thinking** " to win the confrontation larger share of worldly goods, or a revival of community group with neighborhood co-operation to combat such disorders as juvenile delinquency, drug addition, vandalism, crimes and other anti-social vices.

The old man said some of this solutions you mentioned would turn out to be no more than half way measure, in no way reflects on the sincerity of their advocates to people's life. Sincerely speaking, people will do strange things to escape their sense of isolation. They may accept illusions as reality: religiousness without religion, para-social relation with mass-media personalities, to achieve this state is the goal of all. How can you re-order your society and overcome alienation.

The old man said the question you are asking is how it can be done, how such solidarity can be created and sustained in normal times. He said, *the suggestion is a kind of proper orientation and public enlightenment of youth's collectives throughout the world.* What you need is to imbue your members with some sense of higher purpose, but your greatest error would be to assume that such solidarity is merely coerced, although the power to coerce is usually present. If you can do this people will no longer feel alienated. In this process people will sacrifice a meaningless freedom and accept the most terrible discipline in order to feel part of something greater than themselves. But the cure may be fatal if group pressures for conformity become irresistible. **The ultimate problem,** therefore as yet nowhere solved is how to restore and preserve group solidarity without destroying the last remnants of individual autonomy. The alternatives are not pleasant, but on the one hand, a war which may end all life on earth, on the other increasing controls to ensure survival of the society. In the not too distant future, as man multiples at a rapid rate **togetherness** will very likely become more than a figure of speech.

People is possessed of extraordinary powers for good and evil, compelled to make room for new hordes of humanity. In short, caught between the machine and the mass, can they learn to live with themselves and their brothers? Sincerely if there are places or grounds for optimism, surely they are based on the judgment that many of the problems I have discussed with you are transitional, which is part of the very heavy price which your generation has had to pay for their scientific and technological progress. According to my view people's remarkable accomplishments in science and technology can be matched in their social and economic arrangement, but the intelligence that has flourished in the former as yet finds no counterpart in the latter. To close this gap and help people to live with their machines and with themselves thus become the highest goals for every society. These questions are not academic if they are not answered, how the society can meet the direct challenge of a solidarity communism and it is **New Generation!** This is not the place to draw a blueprint for change, yours is a soft and wasteful society. If it ever needed a sense of **National Purpose,** now is the time, but that cannot be achieved or imposed by appointing committees to select goals for you, although this reflects at least dimly an awareness that collective purpose is missing from lives.

Can you arrive at that sense of purpose and retain the freedom you value so highly and use so poorly? Or will you drift into a garrison state that will give you your marching orders? Which shall you choose? I told you before and I have sketched some by no means all of the conditions and influences alienating people in society, can these conditions be altered and alienation overcome? Answers to this question demand the best thinking and planning of which your civilization is capable. They required thinking from the heart as well as the head, they demand co-operation among many diverse groups and among nation. Alienation in society is almost total and that drastic change is called for. As to the danger of nuclear war and mass extermination, the human beast has always lived dangerously invented new and more terrible weapons, for this approach no amount or kind of social planning will succeed in alleviating the situation and on the contrary may make it worse, In short alienation is relative. My son, the rest of the world may not wait long for you to decide Indeed underdeveloped countries at the outer edge of the explosion of population and expectations may learn from the experiences and if they are wise, they should skip the difficult and painful periods of technological adjustment which you experiences now. *Your society should reject a system in which people take from one another more than what they share together.* The integration of society is not a simple task and at best It is imperfectly achieved, or at great cost. But I must confess to you that society which fails to make the effort of eradication is not likely to survive and if citizens of the affluent society feel sorry for themselves let them remember that most people on earth have never tasted any fruit of freedom.

It is like this old man knows much about what I did not know, I told him that I still have many questions to ask.

CHAPTER TWO

THE ORIGIN AND NATURE OF PEOPLE

There is a controversy concerning the nature and origin of people. I explained to him what I learnt from concept. Human beings was regarded as the only creature created by God in the image of God, the creator and the author of universe and life, also to other views, human being are both a biological and a culture being. He is a mammal and belongs to the animal kingdom. Human being unlike most of the other animals has developed brain developed culture as a means of living in the environment for their survival. Human being also regarded as the most remarkable of all creatures in the world who was blessed with some characteristics which other animals do not possess and this accounts for human being uniqueness in the whole world. Therefore the theories of origin of people are sub-divided into three major parts. They are (i) The scientific theory (ii) The religious theory of evolution (iii) The mythical theory of evolution.

The Scientific Theory; the postulated scientific theory is that the solar system originated six million years ago from a cold flat mass of gas and dust was 1.5 million kilometers thick and 9 million kilometers in diameter, and contained great quantities of hydrogen and helium which later condensed and separated into ten flat discs that make up the sun and the nine planets. In conclusion, human being is a mammal, mammals feed their young ones from mammary glands. People also belongs to the order of primates e.g. Gorilla, Apes, Monkeys, Chimpanzees. Man is homosapiens i.e. homo in the division of all colours and races and sapiens species. The general belief of experts in evolutionary theory is that the origin of the ancestor of people who other human being like creatures originated several million years ago is in African continent.

RELIGIOUS EXPLANATION OF EVOLUTION: Religion as belief in the existence of a supernatural ruling power the creator and controller of the universe. Who has given to people a spiritual nature which continues to exist after the death of the body; People believe that evolution of people is connected with God. Many societies also believe that God created human being. Christians belief of creation of special creation which states that God created the earth, light, darkness, water, land, vegetable, sun, star, moon, and living creature and that human being was created last by God in his own image. God put people in the garden of Eden and God made human being to fall asleep one day and removed one of his ribs, closed the flesh back (God, the first surgeon) and he made a woman out of the rib. The man was called Adam and the woman Eve. They became partners to each other.

Muslims also believe strongly in the origin of people in the revelation to Prophet Mohammed. An angel asked him to recite in the name of the (Lord) Allah who created all things and that human being was created out of a clot of blood. In a nutshell, the Quran explanation is that Allah created people last to be the care-taker of all other creatures. Baima who is Adam was the first man, Mahawa who is eve was the first woman. Muslims are of the opinion that God resides in heaven and that He is that creator of human being and other things both living and non-living.

THE MYTHICAL EXPLANATION OF ORIGIN OF PEOPLE: we have a lot of mythical explanation about the evolution or origin of people as there are multi-ethnic groups in the world. Each group claimed their origin in different myths.

My son don't be confused those people who wrote what you just told me now are seekers of knowledge, they are just trying to understand the work of God. To say the fact, the way and when the universe (world) came into being is still a mystery likewise how human being and other living things, both plants and animal of various kinds are created is also a mystery to people up till today.

RELIGIOUS ASPECT OF LIFE: I asked about religion from this old man, he paused for a while and he began the effectiveness of this word cannot be measured in quantitative terms in people's life. But I have a lot to say about this I have mentioned part of this before; I know concerning the origin of people, religion will take close to 90% if you can do the statistical method of analyzing. Meanwhile, have you heard about the illusion and apocryphal of religion. It seems to me uneducated people will believe in illusion of religion while educated somebody will believe in scientific fact which has been tested and proved. A religion is not a group of people; a religion is a system of ideas, beliefs, practices and relationships.

He said further that the central fact of modern history in the modern society, I mean the long period from the end of the middle ages to the present is unquestionably, the issue of religion no doubt the churches, mosques and traditional temples are still very powerful organizations, there are millions of church goers and Muslim followers all over the world up till today there was even considerable talk about a "religious revival" and some popular and patriotic periodicals such as magazine, radio, television, in short the mass media gave a great deal of space to it. Mass media promote a revival of religion, one is only too painfully aware from the nature of this publication that religion is considered as being in the national interest. One could scarcely have a clearer indication of the broader historical fact that in the modern world, the nations as a thoroughly secular institution, outranks any religion.

The warning of religion is a much more concrete and complex fact that a mere change in conscious outlook, it penetrates the deepest strata of man's total psychic life. The loss of the churches, mosques and traditional religion was the loss of a whole system of symbols images dogmas and rites which had the psychological validity of immediate experience and within which hitherto the whole psychic life of modern man had been safely contained in loosing religion man lost the concrete connection with a transcendent realm of being, man was set free to deal with this world in all its brute objectivity. But he was bound to feel homeless in such a world which no longer considered the needs of his spirit. A home is the accepted the needs of his spirit. A home is the accepted framework which habitually contains your life.

Human being became a wanderer upon the face of the earth. Henceforth, in seeking his own human completeness, human being would have to do for themselves what they once had for them unconsciously by the religion through the medium of his sacramental life. Human being was still enthralled by a new and powerful vision and symbols which do not have the immediate and overwhelming reality for you. I must confess to you and to say the fact the whole of nature is merely a canvas upon which the religions symbol and image are painted. Nature and religion, they are unseparated entity. Your leaders can never reveal the avenue where they got their power. History has never allowed people to return to past in any total sense, and your psychological problem cannot be solved by a regression to a past state in which they had not yet been brought into being. On the other hand, enlightened and progressive thinkers are equally blind when they fail to recognize that every major step forward by mankind entailed some loss. Your must have a problem either you like it or not, and this problem has specific time to spend with you when it is time it will go, during the period of that problem, there is nothing you can do unless if the time is up, those enlightened people also have their own problem which they cannot discuss with you. The sacrifice of an older security and the creation and heightening of new tensions. You should bear this in mind against some of the criticisms of existentialism as a philosophy that has unbearable heightened human tensions, it did not create those tensions which were already at work in the soul of modern people, but simply sought to give them philosophic expression, and rather than evading them by pretending they were not there. It is far from true that the passage from the Middle Ages to modern times is the substitution of a rational for a religions outlook.

Human being placed all the weight of their emphasis upon the irrational datum of faith and people was impoverished in order to come face to face with God and the severe and inexplicable demands of their faith. Human being by themselves can do nothing and only God working in us can bring salvation, here the inflation of human consciousness is radically denied and the conscious mind is recognized as the mere instrument and play thing of a much greater unconscious force. Faith is an abyss that engulfs the rational nature of people so long as faith retained its intensity, however, the irrational elements of human nature with accorded recognition and a central place in the total human economics. But as the world moves forward, it becomes more and more secularized in every department of life, faith consequently becomes attenuated, and people begins to look more and more like a gaunt skeleton. A secular civilization leaves them more starkly naked than the reformation had ever dreamed. The more severely they struggles to hold on to the primal face to face relation with God, the more tenuous this becomes, until in the end the relation with God himself threatens to become a relation with nothingness.

But I asked this old man, that, on earth we believe that some people are serving God. He said that is only on my mind, nobody on earth can serve God my son, it is God that is serving you, He makes everything for you especially the nature in order for you to live comfortably, what do you think you can do for God as a being, everyday He cares for you, how much do you think He can ask from you that you can pay, let me elaborate for you either you appreciate him or not, it does not concern God, he has made you and He must care for you. I asked if it is necessary for me to send somebody to God to request something for me, he said that is part of mistakes you have made on earth, God is kind you can talk to Him anytime, any day. He will answer you. But you must give Him a chance to do his work, the problem you have is that you cannot endure, because there is time for everything on earth.

Concerning the issue of the ego that you mentioned, you said it is the beginnings of alienation for people, what can you say about this ego I want more information about this, what this ego is teaching is moral education he wanted people to live in peace, they should not hurt each other. My son the problems people have was that they did not understand his teaching because all he taught them is parable. They asked him so many questions, one of them is concerning death, they asked him and he said one person will be taken and the other person will be left, there may be two women working together, one woman will be taken and the other women will be left, his followers asked him further, where will this be, he answered where there is dead body vultures will always be there, but your people did not understand. Another one is about the kingdom of God, he said God's kingdom is coming but not in a way that you will be able to see with your eyes people will say look God's kingdom is here, don't answered them the kingdom of God is inside you. His followers by that time asked him, why are you teaching people with parable, he said "only you can know the secret of truth about the kingdom of heaven, but other people cannot know these secrets of truth because the person that has will be given more, and he will have even more than he needs. But the person that does not have will lose even the little that he has, that was why I use the parable to teach the people. They will see, but they do not really understand, they also hear but they do not really understand.

What he said, has it not started happening now; where those that have many are still taking form those that have little on earth.

Concerning the issue of Dream: the old man said. Dream a fully crystallized stratification system must distribute dreams as unequally as it distributes other values, if it is to remain unchanged, dreams however not the same as hope are. There can be dream without hope but no hope without dreams. It is very important to imagine the consequences of their separation, they probably appear together when person near the bottom of a stratification system begin to experience some rise in status and learn about others who have risen even further, after a time however, they may run into serious resistance to their further advance. Furthermore, "when everyone agrees, there is very little thinking", most people had been petrified by illusion of religion they have problem they react as if the world is going to an end, instead of facing the reality of life. Most are still waiting for the trumpet to blow so that they can fly and leave this earth, they forget that nobody live on earth without tasting death. Earth is the only galaxy where people can live and survive, there is no other place where he can survive as a being. This is the juncture of contemplating for you, dilemma is very much around.

I said old man you talk about nature I do not think I have any relationship with it. He answered, you said so, in the case of nature no matter your religion you cannot do without nature, such as hill, mountain, sea, air and land. Human being nowadays in the society went to mountain for prayer, they also used sea for baptism, and there are many ways people liaise with nature. Most people will argue that they have nothing to do with it. But for your information, those leaders that you are following know how they pay for nature on behalf of you. Sincerely speaking, you cannot separate nature from religion. It is not necessary for you to contact, touch or feel objects before having a relationship with it, in the day light you can say much about people, but in the night, millions of things occurred that you do not know, but those who engage in it understand better, how they get the power they used. In the area of drugs, the process cannot be done without nature, science and technology, no doubt, have a lot to gain from it, no remedies for that, especially this computer age of yours.

CHAPTER THREE

EDUCATION

Old man, I think education is a better process that somebody can have, because many people have different opinion concerning this. There are many definitions of education as there are institutions and individuals that engage in the business of education. Most of the leading philosophers also contributed their own quota. According to Plato, he defined a good education as consisting in giving to the body and to the soul all the beauty and all the perfection of which they are capable.

Herbert Spencer believes that education has for its object the formation of character. Fredrick Mayer regards education as a process leading to the enlightenment of mankind in intellectual growth, emotional maturity and ethnical awareness.

The sociologists view education as the process of cultural transmission and renewal; this implies that education helps a nation to pass its culture from one generation to another generation with modification.

John Stuart mill is one good example. He suggested, as the core of education the culture which each generation gives to those who are to be its successors. This will enable such successors to keep up to the culture inherited at last, but better still it may enable them to improve on the inherited culture.

Carter good defines education as the art of making available to each generation, the organized knowledge of the past.

Fafunwa believes that education is the sum total of all the processes by which a child or young adult develops the abilities, attitudes and other forms of behaviour, which are of positive value to the society in which he lives. Castle submits that education is what happens to us from the day we are born to the day we die. In his opinion we are being educated all the time, even when many refuse to be taught. It does not even matter whether we attend school or not. We educate ourselves other people or situation or events educate us. We learn from the circumstances in which we live, from the things that surround us. We just cannot help being educated.

Nwosu says education is the lifelong formal and informed processes by which individual learn to live constructively and harmoniously in the society. According to him, education for an individual begins in the womb and end in the tomb. In cyclopedia Americana education is defined as any process by which an individual gains knowledge or insight or develops attitudes or skills, such process may include training, instructing, drilling, initiating, indoctrinating, conditioning, brainwashing or teaching.

But to Sola Olorunda, education is what people intended to learn in order to acquire knowledge which will enable them to possesses skills, value and other valuable things of life and also imbibe positive attitude which cannot be measure in quantitative terms.

In summary, one may say that education has to do with those activities that leads to positive changes in a person in all the spheres of life with the ultimate aim of creating a sound mind in a sound body. The old man responded, my son I think education is supposed to liberate the soul and the body. Concerning education, but to be sincere most of the educators and the education they attained on earth, they had been petrified by illusion of religion, this means level of education does not determine the knowledge someone can acquire on earth as a being. You have got to a certain stage in life where many people believe that wisdom belong of God, because most scholar cannot lead them to their expectation it is like educated people disappointed them in many ways. Concerning the atrocity performed by the educated people, most of the leaders are educated, they failed to deliver the good to the society at large, through the mismanagement of generated income and infrastructural facilities which they fail to distribute equally.

Yours is a time of discrimination, modern people do everything possible to separate themselves in different categories, you have majority and minority, especially the masses, and their interest cannot be preserved in the society to the extent that they lack the sense of belonging. Educated people now engaged themselves in several anti-social vices such as crime, bribery and corruption. But the importance of education can never be over emphasized in modern society. It transformed your society to the extent that most people experience paradise on earth. You can also experience thus also all you need is to get to a stage of self-actualization needs, which psychologist regarded as the highest level of human needs. These includes the needs to know about oneself and the world around; that need to be creative and the need to be a spontaneous, self – motivated achiever.

Some of the characteristics associated with self-actualized persons are:

- They are oriented towards reality

- They accepted themselves for who they are.

- They are spontaneous and unconventional in their thinking

- They are problem centered

-

They are independent.

-

They identified with people

-

They develop intimate relationship

-

They have a good sense of humored

-

They are creative and non-conformist

-

They are democratic

CHAPTER FOUR

SCIENCE AND TECHNOLOGY

Old man, what can you say about this issue of science and technology? He responded, my son workers and consumers, people increasingly alternated by the power of machines which regulate their daily life, even determining their value, the technology which produces machines, however, is but the offspring of a science which has developed the means to transform your planet or destroy it. It has become ever more remote from the lives of ordinary citizens and perhaps the ultimate factor in their alienation. To such citizens, science appears magical and mysterious in its capacity for neutrality toward good or evil. Unfortunately, education has failed to help rising generations of non-scientists to understand science, but the fault lies with the people of science too.

My son, scientists have enjoyed acting the mysterious stranger, the powerful voice without emotion, the expert and the god. Human being is unable to live with and control the extraordinary knowledge and power which their fertile brain has decided. You have been inventing machines at a growing pace now for about one thousand years. This is a short span even in your recorded history, and it is not a thousand part of your history as human being. In that short moment of time, you have found a remarkable indigent into the workings of nature. You have used it to make yourselves far more flexible in your adaptation to the outside world than any other animal has ever being. You can survive in climates which even germs find difficult. You can grow your own food and meat. You can travel overland and you can tunnel and swim and fly all in one body. Sincerely, if any idea wants to be claimed to being called creative, because they have created something then certainly it is the idea of science.

You may think that all that science has created is comfort; it certainly has done that, the very word comfortable. But have you always stop to think about what science has done to your mode of living not to your life? You talk about research for death, the threat of war and the number of peoples who got killed. But have you always weighted this against the increase in your own life span? In the olden days, people has experimented with materials around them to feed, to clothe and shelter themselves. All they does is to find a means of satisfying themselves by providing for their immediate needs. What started as satisfaction of basic needs has now developed into science. Today, the early science work which was merely an assumption of existence of things with priest assertion from churches has been replaced by investigation and empirical tests. Science is becoming a commodity which no nation can afford to neglect; science is a systematic or ordered way of reasoning. Not only have the fact and theories that engage from scientific inquiry affected our beliefs and values, but very methods of going about such inquiry have affected human relationships and society.

Therefore, science can be referred to as human activity embedded in social content which influences the society and in influenced by the society which it serves. Science is also regarded as intellectual activity through which people seeks to understand nature. But in the Middle Ages. The observation and philosophy of the entire scientist at that time were limited in terms of practical terms, because the attitude of the people could not encourage too much investigation since noble men were not required to do manual work but reserved for the slaves. In your society nowadays science is now the alpha and omega, all adoration had been given to science and technology due to the way they transformed your society and natural environment. But the insights of science is not different from that of the arts, science would create values, and discover virtues when it looks into human being, when it explores what makes him human and not an animal and what makes his societies human and not animal packs. You can also reach this unity in your culture, yours is a remarkable age of science. It is for you to use it to broaden and to liberate your culture.

These are the works of science that it is open for everybody to hear, and everybody is free to speak their mind on it. They are marks of the world at its best, and the human spirit at its most challenging. The old man said, my son the question I will kike to pose to you is that science and technology are they creator, destroyer or saviour?

CHAPTER FIVE

SOCIALIZATION

I asked the old man concerning the issue of socialization, how can people socialize? He answered, my son socialization is a process by which an individual learns to behave according to the social traditions and conventions. The human child has a remarkable capacity to imitate others and they develop according to the environment into which they are born. Being a social animal, they tries to win the appreciation of the group in which he lives and hence he naturally tries to imitate the culture of the group. It is through socialization that he is transformed from animal into the human and it is socialization that gives him a balanced personality.

In this your society, imagine what a visitor from outer space might conclude if he attempted to reconstruct the basic quality of human life from a study of a year's headlines and a running tape of a year's newscasts. At the end he would have a long list of stories dealing with murder and theft, fire and crash, riot and skirmish. There would be a few accounts of friendly acts of negotiation of goals accomplished, but the overwhelming impression he would have be one of conflict. How he might conflict. He might wonder how this species manages to survive and even to multiply so rapidly. If he concluded that conflict was a great significance, few of you would be inclined to argue with him. The evidence is too close at hand and too persistent for you to doubt the importance of conflict and in this, I will tell you one of its most common manifestation.

He concluded, a deeper fact of human life is so common that you take it for granted, how many times in the last few days have you counted upon other person, on their values and goals and their actions related to those values and goals for the satisfaction of some need of your own, think not only of family and friends but of strangers, or persons whom you will never meet or know, but who are involved in some chain of activities important to you. I am not referring to generosity and acts of friendship in particular, although these are parts of the situation but to the steady performance of roles into the structures necessary for the achievement of most goals. This is the basic fact with which socialization start. Human beings everywhere live in societies, their interaction is guided to an important degree of norms, by agreed upon rules and procedures.

Each society has designed ways of teaching these norms to each new generation, so that everywhere the human infant, that uncultured barbarian goes through a long process of training of socialization. What they are taught in this process is not necessarily good. When societies are studies comparatively wide variations in their standards and norms, their cultures are clearly revealed from any given value perspective. Therefore, some will be ranked higher than others. But the sociologist acting in this professional capacity does not accept such judgments, although as a private individual, of course he does. He tries to discover what kinds of value are associated with other social facts and with what consequences for human behaviour.

Furthermore, I believe that the original nature of the child is good but it is the society that corrupts him by unnecessary imposition of norms and values. It is his task to observe and explain, not to praise or to blame. He may recall that in certain social groups, patterns of prejudices are taught, children are carefully taught to hate. For most social scientists, objectivity is not an ultimate and final position. It is the position they attempt to maintain during the process of observation and interpretation. For some few, this may be the largest part of life. To study and explain is their basic goal. For most however, the scientific process is part of a larger process, it must be carried out as objectivity as possible in order that it may make its maximum contribution to the human enterprise. An individual scientist may be devoted wholly to the effort to understand some part of nature, but he gains support from the fact that he is part of a larger endeavour that uses increased understanding to achieve some human goal.

Sometimes, a minority group member is seen as hateful and inferior citing an extreme case, one may pull back in revulsion from the violence of a crime committed by some masses in society. You shall simply ask, can they be seen as infants? Was there hatred and violence in them? Did they receives affectionate support from a family? Did the powerful and significant among the dominant group create conditions that gave himself – respect and a sense of justice? You will have little difficulty in asking such questions, the old man said. You had been trying to observe many facts of nature which may profoundly disturb you without losing your desire to study them simply as fact. Once you have some mastery of them, some confidence that your judgments will not be seriously distorted by the fatal combination of ignorance and bias, you can re-introduce your values, you can say without apology. These things I like, those I dislike. Even then, however, you will be wise to pay attention to conditions and processes not to heroes and villains. This is a difficult position to hold on to. Nature abhors not only a physical but a power vacuum. This does not mean of course, that individuals make no difference, it means that their influence is expressed within limits set by major institutional and cultural forces. Those forces do not disappear if you disregard them. By such disregard, you simply reduce your ability to understand the scene before you.

CHAPTER SIX

MAJORITY-MINORITY RELATIONSHIPS

It is important that you be alert to the ways in which they are embedded in the system of social relationship which you call society. I asked the old man how we come about the majority and minority. He said majority were the beneficiary of the infrastructural facilities and social amenities, but minority is a group of people who because of their physical and cultural characteristics are single out from the others in the society in which they live for differential and unequal treatment, and who therefore regard themselves as objects of collective discrimination. But differential and unequal treatment does not necessary mean that one is at the bottom. If two well-trained and competent persons compete for a job of high prestige and income and one losses on the grounds of his group membership alone, this does not indicate a low-class status. A minority is a group which regardless of where it is on the class ladder faces barriers to the pursuit of life's value that are greater that the barriers faced by person otherwise equal qualified. This is a distinction superimposed on the class system.

A member of a minority group is not necessarily in lower class, but he is lower on the stratification ladder not for his group membership. Here, one can think of this as a particular kind of status discrepancy and lack of crystallization. The origin of minorities how does it comes about the members of some groups are set apart for unequally treatment? It is not difficult to imagine why this is done for some individuals. They may have some peculiar talent for antagonizing others, perhaps a perfectly good talent by some standards and thus miss out on that for which they are fully qualified.

But discrimination occurs when all members of a group are treated in a manner that is in violation of accepted standards, no matter what characteristics they possess as individuals. The origin of this practice is to be found in the appearance of heterogeneous societies. Through most of people's history, the first several hundred thousand years, years of it, they lived in small, homogeneous societies. All members spoke the same language, practice the same religion, were the same of physical type, and followed the same customs. A few thousand years ago this situation began to change as a result of migration and conquest groups which are different in important ways came into continuous contact. Under some circumstances they are formed into larger structure, nations and empires. Their former identities however, frequently remained. Conquerors and conquered tribes clung to their own customs and religion, the sacred ways of their fathers racial lines remained, memories of an earlier day when they had been independent stood as barriers against loss of group identity. Today, both migration and the process of forging larger societies continue to create minorities. There is scarcely a society in the world today that does not have within it one or more groups, different in language, religion, race, or culture which are in some measure underprivileged.

By now, you have doubtless asked yourself why are societies so universally stratified? Mankind seems to be so experimental about almost everything when one views societies comparatively, that it may seem surprising that there are not several societies that distribute income, power and prestige equally, or if not equally, at least give each infant an equal chance to compete for them, when social scientific find a universal structure, they are likely to wonder, what function does it perform? Viewing stratification in this way, it is necessary to get various necessary societal job done. My son, "talent is scarce", certain critical jobs which are also difficult might be neglected if capable individual were not motivated to perform them.

To stress that social life in characterized to an important degree by reciprocal expectations is not to deny that there are problems, conflicts and disagreements in perspective, against the background of social order. This statement requires some interpretations. It scarcely need arguing that all societies have problems, hunger, disease, natural disasters, interpersonal conflict. Modern complex societies have reduced some of these, although they have increased others, but they are faced with a still different types of problems. The basic principle here is that "social problems have social origin, in the sense that they involve disagreement among members of the group in question over means or end". But "if the cure is worse than the disease, we do not send for the doctor".

I told this old man that, I am really more concerned on how modern societies can live in peace, if they cannot, he should tell me another place to go and he said your world is the only known planet in which human being live, it is one world divided into seven main geographical land masses called continents.

Each continent is composed for sovereign and independent territories. Each independent nation states grants citizenship to its people, has it political system and government, purpose its own economic goals and propagates its own brand of ideology. The continent of the world do not exist in complete isolation from each other. The nation-state which are the main unit of a continent have to carry on some of their activities in the world environment, thus they not only come into contact with each other on their continents, but they also interact with nation-states in other continents.

The word wide interaction take place in what you call the international system. The nature of the relation of states reflect the nature of the international system. The main feature of the international system is anarchy. Unlike the nation-state system the international system lacks a control authority to regulate activities and arbitrate between the conflicting interests of nation-states, which constitute the main units operating within it. Thus the relation which nation-states have with each other are characterized by conflict and cooperation. Therefore, in the international system, power consideration are of immense importance, the ability of each state to use its power to self-defense will determine its sovereignty and effective participation in the international system.

A state has to rely on its own power in conducting its relation with other sovereign states. Where its own power is inadequate, it might find it necessary to enter into an alliance with any one or more states with which cooperation would be more beneficial. But cooperation in the international system today does not preclude conflict tomorrow, and vice-versa. But a lot of activities and international organization were put together to unite people in the world such as United Nations Organization (U.N.O.), African Union (A.U), Economic Community of West African States (ECOWAS), IMF, UNESCO, UNICEF and many others. Especially sports is one of the basic element that promote unity in society. It has contributed immensely to cooperation and coming together among people in the world. During any organized competition people come together regardless of their race, ethnicity, color or religion.

So also, the effort of international organization can never be over emphasized in your modern society, they make peace and create room for co-existence among the people in the world. Although, as I mentioned earlier that proper orientation and public enlightment of youths can make you realized the awareness and co-existence within the modern society. Above all is **love** through this you can do everything together to wipe out the source of poverty in your society. Modern people with modern problems, new-generation, this is the time for you to realized yourselves and seek for reality of life. There is need for you to converge and convince yourselves on the rational for your commonness. Your rulers must however, remember that if they appear to make peaceful change impossible, they are preparing volatile ground to make violent change inevitable.

But, new generations, how long would you stay to proclaim your public acclamation? Modern society should stop discrimination among the races in the world and society at large because you have the same origin, your environment is what makes you different in color.

CHAPTER SEVEN

WHO ARE YOU?

At this juncture, you this old man have told me a lot concerning my feelings but who are you personally? He responded, I am the knowledge who stands as a mystery for people on earth, those who seek for me can see me. But who is God? God is the positive thinking of human endeavour, He stays every-where. But some people on earth are saying that they are working for God and you said God is every-where. You are supposed to know those who work for God, they died peacefully not in agony or frustration. As individuals, how can we moved with God? I mentioned this earlier, your lackadaisical attitude is what chased you away from God and your stratification from God begins with money and power, they are the genesis, if you want to move with God, what you need is faith. Is it necessary for me to pray to God, yes pray to Him and praise Him, for what He has done for you. He does not required anything from anybody. But some people fail to pray to God, but they still get all they need. It is possible, my son, there is a **Devine Power** for everybody on earth, either you pray or not, when it is your time, you will get what you desire. What are we supposed to ask from God?

These two things are major and necessary, God, give me what is good for me and remove all bad things from my life, simple. Can we ask for money from God? He answered, that is the place where you made mistakes you forget that you made money yourself, for easy transaction of your business. It does not concern God.

Who is the man we called Satan on earth? He explained, you called him Satan does God created anybody as Satan, don't you know that all the negative attitudes of human endeavors is what you called Satan. What about the one mentioned in the scripture, I told you earlier that, they are all seekers of knowledge. What really killed human beings, and he said the major two things that killed man is **terminal disease and human error**, he explained further everybody has his own terminal disease from the day he is born as a being, it now depends on how he takes care of himself , what of human error? Human error is what you invented for yourselves due to your over-civilization and inordinate ambition, such as vehicle, airplane, ship, and other sophisticated weapons, and now-a days what you consumed is 90% of chemicals, this weaken your flesh and terminates your life, he said.

Life after death I have been hearing about this argument, what can you say about this. He said, when you die that is the end you cannot know your destination again, the only way you can come back to this earth is through **reincarnation,** it means the perfection of your soul, in order to atone for your sins committed on earth. I asked, what of the animals can they come back as a being? He said it is not possible for animals to come back as a being. I asked the old man concerning the issue of human error, how vehicle, airplane, ship and other sophisticated weapons has been used to terminated people's life, and he said, road accident occurred because of over-speeding of many drivers, they wanted to make huge money within few hours, and most of them will not repair their vehicles at the appropriate time or service it at the right time. In case of airplanes, there are many air-crafts that are supposed be condemned or abandoned, because of money, they will still be forcing it to work, that kind of air-craft can crash anytime. So also in the area of seaport, people in modern society has been in danger over their invention for survival.

I also asked the old man concerning the allegations leveled against the months of September to December, that a lot of bad incidents occurred during this period, and he said all days are equal before God, he said towards the end of the year, individual struggle to make money for the incoming festival, what they supposed to do within a week they will try it for one day, this lead to many bad incidents in every aspect of people's life. He also said endurance is what we need to live in this modern society.

I asked the old man about the witches and wizards how they get the power they are using, and he said every power is from God and supernatural, God gave them power in order to enhance the human activities on earth, but your people misused this power especially in African society. They used this power to delay progress, afflicts many people with diseases, kill people mysteriously by this power instead of helping the society by using this power to ensure progress for individual and for the nation. To say the fact, developed countries grabbed this opportunity given to them by God, they used this power to develop themselves in many areas, majorly in science and technology, and they live comfortably and experience paradise on earth. African countries should learn from these developed countries and make use of this power to develop themselves also, but if they fail to, they will continue to live in abject poverty. Being ignorant of these powers does not allow the detection of many talents, which is why for those that make it from African, it is by God's grace and power. Those witches and wizards forget that destination can be changed but destiny cannot be changed.

CHAPTER EIGHT

INORDINATE AMBITION

I asked the old man on the issue of inordinate ambition. He said this issue has led to many things in modern society. It is through this that we come across the armed robbery and several immorality sagas. The case of armed robbery is disastrous to humanity, this caused by inordinate ambition of people especially the youths that engaged themselves in various anti-social vices, and they are using sophisticated weapons to frustrate the lives of the people. What caused this was that they have odd personality and they cannot wait for their time, they want to acquire property by force, through this they died at the early stage of their lives, some are awaiting trial why some are sentenced to various years in prison. Youths of nowadays cannot endured at all. The old man said, the issue of sex is very common in your modern society, especially the way adolescents practice sex, what led them to this and how people have turned prostitution into a profession.

Sex is sexual activity and everything connected with it, sexual expression on the other hand is meant for two principal reasons which are (i) procreation (b) for mere enjoyment or self-satisfaction. Who is an adolescent, Adolescents are baby fathers or baby mothers who indulged in sexual intercourse without the ability to shoulder or bear its responsibilities. On the other hand an adolescent is a person going through the transaction period. That is from childhood to adulthood which is often referred to as adolescence. Simply put adolescence is that period in every person's life that lies between the end of childhood and the beginning of adulthood. Girls usually begin the adolescent period a year or two earlier than boys. Many lower class youth drop-out of secondary schools before graduation and leave home. Some even set up families of their own by the time they are seventeen or eighteen. This is a result of laxity of normal sexual habit among the adolescent. Adolescence can be both biological and social in nature.

The beginning of adolescence is marked by biological changes in the adolescent. As a matter of fact, just before puberty, this occurs what is known as a pre - adolescent growth spurt. It takes place in girls mostly during the age of 9 - 11 years and in boys between 11 and 14 years. Prior to this time, the rate of growth in height and weight as been slowing down. Now for a period of two or three years, the rate is greatly accelerated during this period and following shortly thereafter, the secondary sexual characteristics emerged in girls. First, the rounding of the hips, breast appearance, pubic hairs and onset of menstruation. In boys, some of secondary sexual characteristics the mark the beginning of adolescence and the appearance of pubic hair, facial hair, voice change, broken voice, and night emission. All these are biological included. Girls look more beautiful and more inviting during this period. The end of the adolescence for both girls and boys is marked largely by social changes and criteria. He explained further that society is experiencing an eye - sore concerning the attitudes of these adolescents, towards sexual relations. In the society, hardly can one avoid a discussion on sexual immorality of these young ones on a daily basis, let alone the weekly papers, even the monthly magazines are not left out in the publication of adolescent sexual habits.

Adolescent boys and girls discuss the practice sex at will, anywhere, anyhow, along the street, in the campuses, at market places, in classrooms, in uncompleted buildings not to mention film houses, cinema halls or hotels. Another instance is when boys gather and contribute some amount which is agreed upon purposely to organize a night party just to catch fishes. During such a get together, boys chatter up girls and without wasting time, they become regular bedmates. There is another case where in some young ones would gather themselves together to form clubs, and through that, they make sexual expression legal among themselves. The issue of sexual attitudes of adolescents in societies has marital problems, rampant abortion, barrenness, problem of the choice of future partner, school drop – out.

Due to independence from parents and other authority figures, an adolescents engages in activities which are contrary to the values and rules of their society. Adolescents suffer from a variety of developed mental difficulties and they try to formulate the life styles that make them highly anxious and enable them to tolerate frustration, so they turn to drugs or strictly get advices from their live group in order to overcome the stress.

Locally, not all behavior is motivated, not all behavior is determined by basic needs. Some responses or series of responses are tripped off by isolated stimuli and are the products of conditioning or complex habit hierarchies or even instinct or other innate response pattern.

The issue of attitude is the intention to perform a particular operation. It is the immediate response to present stimuli and unmoving from one step to another. The mechanism of attitude is more likely to be at work. Attitude operates within brief stretches of behaviour, perhaps, the meaning which is most obviously relevant to the explanation of the direction and control of thought is one covered by the term **attitude**. Attitude or frame of mind can be either conscious or unconscious either international or motor readiness. Adolescence is a period of increasing awareness about social adaption, during this period the child develops attitude, beliefs and norms about social stimulation and group cohesiveness. They are concerned about the comments of peers, parent and adult in the society, they want to be recognized as such, social stimulation helps to develop the adequacy of the way they perceive themselves, that is self-concept they may be more loyal to the peers group on many issues.

(Determine Sexual Attitudes.) An attitude is the key factor in attention, concentration and selection of appropriate stimuli in the course of a task. Nowhere, perhaps is the gap between the everyday world as experience and understood by individuals and that world as measured an analyzed by sociologists as apparent as in the realm of sexual behaviour within an ideology where woman are seen as object of lust. Sex is something different from the relation between human beings but a matter of conquest and achievement for the male individual. Women of easy virtues, place no moral justification on how where and when to introduce sex, especially where values are placed on going to bed for the sake of it.

Factors responsible for the current sex revolution can easily be identified as urbanization, quest for education and industrialization. A situation which remove youths so early in life from parental and community authority and control also facilitate unhealthy liberal attitude to sex in society. Cultural differences among the ethnic groups are glaring but notwithstanding the issues of sex discussion is usually cloaked with taboos and superstition.

In religious doctrines, such discussion is generally considered sacrilegious, unethical and sinful, these attitudes and behaviour are jealously guarded by culture and the doctrines of religion, politics and even law. Children even infants are sexually in their fashions, not only do they respond pleasurably to warm baths and baby – oil but one of the earliest thing a baby boy does after the first cry is to have an erection: the baby-girls vagina lubricates within 24hours of birth. Masturbation and almost unmistakable signs of orgasm have been identified by observers for boys and girls babies under one year old. Many men and some women testify that their first remembered masturbation to orgasm happened at four or five years of age. Today in societies adolescents no longer adhere to cultural regulation regarding sex. There are doubts to existence of ideal virginity at marriage as a moral code in contemporary societies. It is being speculated that despite cultural sanction, virginity at marriage of both male and female partners which use to be regarded as a virtue traditionally is now becoming a social taboo. Lots of issues are involved in the sexual life of human beings; the problem of marriage, marital life, pre-marital sex and extra marital sexual affairs, divorce, abortion, prostitution, sexually transmitted diseases (S.T.D) and family planning are associated with sexual life of people today.

Adolescents Sexual Attitudes (A.S.A) learning to be a heterosexual person will not take place in a vacuum, opportunities must be provided for learning and the adolescent must have the motivation necessary to take advantage of the opportunity given. The environment conditions are essential to the successful establishment of heterosexual relationship. First, there must be a sufficient number of members of the opposite sex of appropriate age, intellectual status and personality adjustments available to give the adolescents an opportunity to select congenial companion and have pleasurable social contact with them. Secondly, there must be an encouraging, sympathetic and helpful attitude on the parts of parents and other adults, be an environment in which sexes are segregated not only increases the adolescent difficulties in making heterosexual social contact but, what is more damaging is that it tend to develop in the adolescent a feeling of inadequacy in situations involving members of the opposite sex.

Transition to adult sexuality involves more than physical changes that occur at puberty for the adolescents must develop new interests and attitudes and learn new patterns of behaviour, normally, "adult" sexuality means heterosexuality in which sexual interest and affection are focused on members of the opposite sex. In early adolescence, sexual feelings and drives are diffused and can be fixed on anyone or anything, the adolescent has an emotional attachment for how these feelings and drives will be expressed depending largely on learning and the influence of social pressures. Not until the diffuse of sexual feelings and drives are focused on members of the opposite sex and it leads to patterns of behavior normally associated with these feelings and drives. Can the adolescent be considered at heterosexual person or one who as achieved adult sexuality?

Heterosexual interest in childhood is expressed primarily in composition in adolescence by contrast. It is accompanied by a strong desire to win the approval of members of the opposite sex.

In early adolescence, this is romantic interest is expressed in erotic day dreams, talking about sex and members of the opposite sex, concern about appearance and crude ways of showing off to attract the attention of members of the opposite sex. The girls may become shy in the presence of their former boy pals. They may "moan" over the pictures of popular motion pictures actors or television stars. Little cliques of pre-adolescent girls may display silly, gigging attitude in the presence of boys or may seem to evince an attitude of superiority to boys to boys of their own age, later, this interest shows itself in a desire to dance to have dates and to engage in other social-sexual activities.

I asked the old man concerning the conditions contributing to sexual attitudes, and he said, sexual attitude in influenced by the glandular condition of the individual Gonald insufficiency delays the development of sexual responsiveness. Testosterone stimulates responsiveness in both males and females. Pituitary and thyroid differences inhibit sexual responsiveness, social factors largely determine how heterosexually will be expressed. Sine a strong how drive is commonly regarded as sign of masculinity, adolescent boys are motivated to engage in all kinds of heterosexual behaviour. Girls who look upon marriage as a way of establishing themselves as woman are predisposed to date and engage in expression of love at an earlier age than girls who find other avenue of self-expression rewarding. "Being in love as teenager appears in some cases to be escape for those who fell that other door to the future are closed".

Adolescence is that age when all human characteristic features show everything for the girls in the eyes of boys, in the body system glitters like gold, in girls especially attention is highly directed to body treatment even when feeling as a bit odd, the flesh will respond to treatment and the beauty will show. These are symptoms of attraction; boys are objective, impendent, competitive, adventurous, self-confident and ambitions. You can hear girls when they are out of sight whispering it jealously. True, the paddy is nice, on the other hand, the girls are dependent, passive, subjective but very tactful, gentle aware of the feelings of others and able to express tenderness and emotion often but not always. Boys do not hide admiring the opposite sex body beauty even publicly "yeah girl" you are just too much, you "fine" where and when both side discover eyeing one another. If youthfulness is a symptom of attraction, wears and outfit is another attractive stimulant.

Girls are usually not attracted, their basic needs are love and security; but boys are attracted. "But it is right for girls to look feminine, you will like them that way. They look better if they look feminine, soft, and womanly. Female, not denying one's sex some girls wear trousers, sometimes, they are pretty. African woman, they always think of that as femininity with their round bottoms and big legs".

Adolescence exploration is testing the validity of taboos of don'ts in their life and ascertaining their genders motivate heterosexual behaviour. Sometimes, boys use it as ego boosting. Mass media focus the adolescent's attention on the importance of heterosexual relationship in the culture. Popular songs, movies, television and literature help the role of lover or loved one to learn patterns of romantic behaviour.

Male sexuality, boys respond to stimuli more and are more easily aroused sexually than girls. While the reasons for these differences have not been fully determined the following speculations are commonly given. Boys have a stronger innate sex drive, the sensory capacity for stimulation is greater in boys and the socio-sexual acculturation of boys is such as to encourage them to respond more openly to sexual feelings and drive of their speculation. When a man sees a woman; those body build up or physique is attractive that serves as a kind of sex appeal and the man develops interest in the woman. Apart from physique, the exposures of certain features in a woman because of her mode of dressing could features in a woman students reported more sexual aroused, interest and pleasure whereas female students reported disgust. Men tended to have more dreams involving sexual arousal and climax than woman.

Female sexuality, in the female, sex hormones appear to have little influence on the degree of sexual responsiveness, yet since her conduct emanates from biochemistry, her sexual responsiveness is not totally devoid of some hormone basic, however small. In the female, the genesis of sexual responsiveness appears in their desire for attention and for the affection of male. Her sexuality is strongly based on the social attractiveness the male has for her. The anatomy of the male do not excite woman sexually in most cases. However, the attention of the male, association with the male and the expression of affection by the male can give arousal to the woman.

The woman wants male attention, she wants the embrace and the affection of the man, and still, most women are apprehensive and even fearful of men about one third of female have a sex drive that exceed that of the male. They are capable of respected sexual climax, of which no male. They are capable of respected sexual climax, of which no male is capable. A woman may take pleasure in her power to arouse male but if she, in her power arouses and the man rejects her, she can plan a dangerous game. Women were significantly more conservative with respect to alternative life-styles than the men were.

Females are on the averages, less readily arouses sexually than males are and that they do not seem to feel the need for sexual intercourse as often as men. It is further shown that while adolescent girls are more interested in love and security rather sexual intercourse. Most male adolescents are more interested in sexual intercourse, and they developed sexual attitude through these forms of sexual activity to the heterosexual relationship, such as kissing, deep kissing, and breath stimulation over the clothes, breast stimulation under the clothes, genital opposition and sexual intercourse. The solution to curb prostitution and other pre-marital activities in the modern society what we discussed had far reaching implications for the sexual attitude of the adolescents in generals. Unemployment had led many ladies to prostitutions to say the fact, solution is that in the home, parents should show good examples to their children especially adolescents who are aiming to attain the period of adulthood. That

They should enlighten them concerning sex and let them know the implication of casual sex, they should let them realize that abstinence is safety. In the school teacher is supposed to be a role model for the students, in this way they should also include sex-education into the curriculum right from the primary schools, secondary schools also in the other institution of learning. Public address systems should equally be used to educate your illiterate populace. This will enable them to acquire more knowledge concerning practicing sex because awareness removes ignorance. Finally, Guidance and counselors should be available in the school systems so that they will be able to guide the students and also counsel them, particularity those female who seek for love and security from their male counterpart, because majority of male prefer sexual intercourse rather than love and security.

Guidance and counseling inside and outside the school will enable them to live up to the apex of their ability and capability, it will also not allow unwanted pregnancy to be a barrier between their achievement and potentiality.

From this juncture, I now remember my country Nigeria that the present -day adolescents are frivolous and way – ward. To say the fact, the sexual attitude of Nigeria adolescent is an eyesore. In the past decades, virginity at marriage for both males and females is as important as the air we breathe in Nigeria. Any woman that loses her virginity before marriage is sent back to her parents in shame and the blame is share among every members of such bride's family. Simply put, males and females are not expected to lose their virginity before they are legally married. Also, it has been discovered that 56% of Nigeria's population is below 20 years and the median age at first sexual intercourse for girls is 16. Teenagers have accounted for 80% in safe abortion complications and 60% of youth do not know that pregnancy is possible at first intercourse.

CHAPTER NINE

WHY SECRET CULTS?

Why secret cults exist and why is it rampant among students in society, in every human society there is the need for a group of people to come together to protect a common interest as the creator made for human to make life more meaningful to them. In this, we come across the formation of associations, unions and clubs. Human being are not an island, so also human beings are regarded as gregarious animal for the fact that they love to live in group and also interact in many ways.

It is in this trend that the students formed groups which they thought would serve their interest well.

Cultism, a system of religious worship. It is a closed association and clubs of restricted membership and mysterious activity; it can be defined as a group of people coming together with the same common interests for the same common goals. They are secret in the sense that membership is usually restricted and are not publicly known. These clubs are instituted by a group of close associated, for the preservation, promotion of moral social ideals on the campuses, they enforce and maintain discipline, justice and regulate social and moral attitudes and behaviour. The members claim to possess knowledge and consider themselves superior in knowledge and ability to enforce law and order within a given campus, executive members are constituted by cult members. They share common objectives and strive to attain common goals, in sanitizing the students' community and protect individuals from the least of embarrassment or harassment. Viewed along this perspective cultism was not intended to be evil, rather, it existed for the well-being of the students community.

Furthermore, in the contemporary community, secret cults have gone dangerous and disturbing, they now engage in various anti-social behaviour. They committed murder and looting and make use of deadly sophisticated weapons.

From here I remember my country Nigeria for instance, the Nigeria Tribune Newspaper of Tuesday, October 13, 1992 reported on a wee cult at university of Ibadan. It disclosed that a student of the U.I. was confirmed dead in a violence involving members of three secret cults in the campus, when Eye and Black Axe were in farces, but the latter got upper hand thus members of eye from Ilato polytechnic joined forces to reinforce their fellows including those at (LASU) using guns and killed Kunle Adegboro and Olugbenga Oyeniyi both final year students, while Olorieye (Speaker of the house) final year political science student was shot in the legs, Femi bright a 400 level history student was found bleeding from various matched cuts.

The case of raping a 16 years old female medical student of University of Ibadan to death by cult member while on her way to the lecture theatre is also worthy or mentioning. At the Federal Polytechnic Bida, 3 students were jailed in July 1997.

They were all said to be members of Eye confraternity. The 1999 Obafemi Awolowo University Saga. During which the life of one of the students Popularity known as African and Sabo including the secretary general of the students union is still very fresh in our memory.

More so, I got to know reliably that the pirate's confraternity was formed in 1952 at the then University collage, Ibadan by seven students of the University. The students included Wole Soyinka, Ralph Opara, Olumuyiwa Awe, Ikphere Aigimonkuede, Pius Olegbe, Nathaniel Oyelola, and Ifagbale Amater. At that time, the cult was motivated by the necessity of breaking the colonial strong – holds on African by adopting unconventional methods to check the excess of the colonial lectures in the university, to say the fact "the lapse of time is capable of working wonders on both mental and the physical being of anyone", the issue of eradicating of cult activities in the society is a mere talking shop because those people in position of power are involved in cultism. They financed the cult members in order to attain higher posts or political appointments. I think that, those students who involve themselves in cultism are those with deviant behaviours. They lack moral education and sense of belonging.

However, it is difficult to say, what is impossible for the dream of yesterday is the hope of today and reality of tomorrow society needs to implement this ideology in order to achieve their aim towards cultism, including organization of seminar and talks to educate students at all levels of educational sectors is highly advocating, for student should be their brother's keeper in place by fellow student.

Furthermore students should be taught how to cultivate positive personality that can expose them to godly injunction that will aid peace in all schools. Lastly, parents and guardians should be vigilant on their words so as to curb any unlawful attitude of their children to humanity. With all these ideas you can re-order your society and orientate youth concerning this issue, they are the leaders of tomorrow, take good care of them.

CHAPTER TEN

THE HOUSE OF GOD

I asked this of old man concerning the house we build on earth that we called house of God, and he replied, my son you have a shallow thought, don't you remember in the scripture, when they said God cannot live in the house they build with hand, I told you before that he lives everywhere, but all those **rapacious agents of little virtue** will not declare to you because of what they will achieve, if men were God, it will be very difficult for you to live on earth. Do not be deceived my son, this world is equifinality, no beginning on end, people live and people die. But the earth continues forever. All things continue the way they have been since the beginning. The same things will be done as you have always been doing it. There is nothing new in this life. People might say look this is new, but that thing has always been there. It was here before you were. People do not remember the things that happened long age. In the future, people will not remember what is happening now, and later, other people will not remember what those people before them did.

My son, trying to become wise is like trying to catch the wind, more wisdom more frustration and more sorrow. All that you worked for, the people that lived after you will get those things, you will not be able to take those things with you. Some other person will control everything you worked and studies for and you do not know if that person will be wised or foolish.

This is also senseless, and I asked him with all these, what am I going to do and he answered. The best things you can do is eat, drink and enjoy the work you do, this come from God, if you do good and please God then God will give you wisdom, knowledge and joy. God gave you the ability to think about his world, but you can never completely at the right time. The best thing for you to do is to be happy and enjoy yourselves as long as you live because God want every person to eat, drink and enjoy his work. These are gifts from God. Everything that God does will continue forever. You cannot add anything to the work of God and also you cannot take anything away from the work of God. God did this so people would respect him.

God has planned a time for everything, and God has planned a time to judge everything people do. God will judge the good people and the bad people on earth. But I asked this old man about what people have said concerning the punishment of sin, they believed that God will not judge on earth, the old man responded, I said before that you have a shallow thought my son, have you ever seen anybody sin on earth without punishment before he/she left, nobody lived on earth and sin without being punished and the greatest punishment for sin is death. You are a human being, your life is short and full of trouble. People's life is like a flower that grow quickly and then dies away. People's life is like a shadow that is here for a short time and then it is gone and his destination they knew they know no more. People's life is limited". There is hope for a tree if it is cut down, it can grow again. It will keep sending out new branches. Its roots might grow old in the ground and its stump die in the dirt, but with water it will grow again. It will grow branches like a new plant. But when people dies, they are gone. You could take all the water from the sea, until the rivers all run dry, and the human will still be dead. When a person dies, he lies down and he doesn't get up. The sun will go down and disappear and a dead person will not wake up and they will not wake him up from that death.

God want people to see that they are like animals. Is a human better than an animal? No! Why? Because everything that happens to animals also happen to human, they die in the same way, and they have the same breath. The body of human and animals end the same way. They came from the earth and in the end they will go back to the earth. Who knows what happen to the spirit of a human? Who knows if a people's spirit goes up to God while an animal's spirit goes down into the ground? You should not worry about the future why? Because no one can help you see what will happen in the future, and a mere lover of gold will not be satisfied with gold, neither any lover of wealth with income.

Finally, "The love of money is the root of all sorts of injurious things on earth. Human is a frivolous and incongruous creature, their worst defect is the perpetual obliquity from the day of Adam till today, and everything that happened to human on earth, they caused it by themselves.

THE TIME

I asked the old man concerning this issue and he responded that, man is deeply conscious of the passing time. With each tick of the clock, he progresses a step further down time's corridor. He is wise, indeed, if he makes proper use of his time. To say the fact, for everything, there is an appointed time, even a time for every affair under the heaven; a time for birth and a time to die, a time to plant and a time to uproot what was planted, a time to kill and a time to heal, a time to break down and a time to build; a time to weep and a time laugh. How fleeting is time! God himself lives in an eternity of time. As for his creatures, it has pleased him to set them in the stream of time. Time and unforeseen occurrence befall them all. Happy is the person who at all times includes God in his thoughts and who welcomes God's provision of food at the proper time. Though time is universal, no human living is able to say what it is. It is as unfathomable as space. No one can explain where the stream of time began or where it is flowing. These things belong to the limitless knowledge of God.

On the other hand, time has certain characteristics that can be understood. Its apparent rate of flow can be measured. Time moves in one direction only. Like traffic on one way street, time moves relentlessly in that one direction, forward, ever forward. Wherever the speed of its forward movement, time can never be thrown into reverse. You live in a momentary present. However, this present is in motion flowing continually into the past. There is no stopping it.

THE PAST

The past is gone. It is the history, and it can never be repeated. Any attempt to call back the past is as impossible as trying to make a waterfall tumble up-hill or an arrow fly back to the bow that shot it.

Your mistakes have left their mark in the stream of time, a mark that only God can wipe out. In like manner, a person's good deeds in the past have made a record that will come back to him, with blessings from God. The past has been won or lost. No longer is there any control over it and the wicked it is written for like grass they will speedily wither, and like green new grass, they will fade away.

THE FUTURE

The future is different. It is always flowing toward you. By the help of God's word, you can identify obstacles that loom ahead of you and prepare to meet them. You are interested in the wise use of time, as it affects that future.

TIME INDICATORS

Your modern-day watches and clocks are time indicators. They serve as rulers for measuring time. In similar manner, God the creator, has set in motion giant time indicators, the earth spinning on its axis, the moon revolving around the earth, and the sun, so that from their standpoint on earth, people may be accurately advised of the time. As a multitude of objects with interlocking purposes, these heavenly bodies move in their perfect cycles, unendingly and unerringly measuring the one-directional movement of time.

THE DAY

As the earth makes one complete rotation on its axis, it measures out one day of 24 hours. In this sense, a day is made up of day time and night time, a total of 24 hours. However, the day light period itself usually average to 12 hours, is also called day. Day refers to a period of time contemporaneous with some outstanding person.

THE HOUR

The division of the day into 24 hours is traced to Egypt. Your modern-day division of the hour into 60 minutes originated from

Babylonian mathematics, which was a sexagesimal system based on the number 60.

THIS WEEK

It was early in history that man began to count his days in cycles of seven.

THE SEASONS

In preparing the earth for habitation, God made the wise and loving provision of the seasons. These follow as a consequence of the earth's being tilted, at a 23.5^0 angle to the plane of its travel around the sun. This results in first, the southern hemisphere's and then six months later, the northern hemisphere's being tilted toward the sun, so that the season proceed in order.

This change of the season provides for variety and contrast and controls the times for planting and harvesting. This arrangement for change and contrast of the seasons through the year is to continue forever. For all the days the earth continues, seed sowing and harvest, and cold and the heat, and summer and winter, and day and night will never cease.

THE YEAR

The year mean "repeat" and carries the ideal of a cycle of time. This was appropriate, since each year, the cycle of seasons was repeated. An earthly year is the time it takes for the earth to make one complete revolution, or trip around the sun. the actual time that it takes for you here on earth to complete this trip is 365 days 5 hours 48 minutes 46 seconds, or approximately 365 ¼ days. This is called the true solar year.

HOW TIME MOVES FASTER

"There is an old saying that a wretched kettle never boils". It is true that when you are watching time, when you are conscious of it, when you are waiting for something to happen, and then it seems to pass ever so slowly. However, if you are busy, if you are interested in and preoccupied with what you are doing, then it really appears that "time flies". Moreover, with older people time seems to pass much more quickly than with young children why is this? One year added to the life of one - year old means a 100 percent increase in life's experiences. One year added to the life of a 50 year old means just 2 percent more. To the child a year seems a long time. The older person if busy and in good health finds that the years seem to fly faster and faster. He comes to a deeper understanding that there is nothing new under the sun. On the other hand, young people still have the seemingly slower, formative years with them. Instead of striving after wind with a materialistic world, they may use these years profitably in pilling up a wealth of Godly experience.

TIME WHEN PEOPLE LIVE IN PEACE

There are joyous days ahead that will be far from calamitous it's for lovers of righteousness, the time there will be no more idleness. Illness, boredom and vanity will have vanished. There will be work to do, absorbing and intriguing, calling for expression of people's perfect abilities and bringing intense satisfaction in accomplishment. The year will seem to flow faster and faster, and appreciative and retentive minds will be continually enriched with memories of happy events. As millenniums pass, human on earth will be doubt come to appreciate more fully God's view of time, for a thousand years in God's eyes are but as yesterday when it is past. Viewing the stream of time from your present human standpoint and taking into account God's promise of a new world of righteousness, how joyous in prospect are the blessings of that day, for there God commanded the blessing to be even life to time indefinite. This can occur when people begin to live in peace and stop discrimination among the races in the world and distribute income equally. *Being optimistic in the faces of adversity is a powerful secret weapon.*

AGE

I asked the old man concerning age and he said, this refers to chronological numerical stage in one's life time. Human learns best in the first seven years of life, it is otherwise referred to as critical period. This is because the brain is at its best then. It is the period of pliability when a child can be bent, a period when child's character can be molded. The period of 18 – 19 years, the old man called this radical period, it is a period of assimilating to imbibing the cultural system of environment. Most youths misuse this period, they want to be socialized at all cost, and through this they put themselves in palaver. At the age of 20, the individual is getting more experienced. Age 40 is regarded as realism age, the best of production due to experience.

A period when people reach the peak of their lives is 60 years. At period, their memories may start failing, they may have senile amnesia, they forget things easily, their short term memory sensory channel is at fault, they use more of the long term memory sensory channel. It is however, assumed that for people who use the brain in academic pursuit, it takes a long time before they can reach the stage of regressions, a stage when the individuals adopt childish behaviours.

The age of a people influences their need, occupation, and the pattern of public expenditure on them. Their age groups are normally recognized.

(i)

Children who are under 15 years are infants and adolescents. This group is largely non-reproductive and increasingly non-reproductive and they are generally referred to as dependent population. In many developing countries, almost half of the population is in this group. Meanwhile in developed countries, there has been a marked tendency for the proportion in this group.

(ii)

Adults who are between 15 and 64 years. This is sometimes sub-divided for further analysis into young adults 15 – 35 years and older adults 35 – 64 years. The adult age group particularly those in the age group of 15 – 49 is the most reproductive and productive and supports the bulk of the other two groups. It is also the most mobile age group.

(iii)

The aged who are 65 above. There is a marked majority of females who are mostly non - productive and include a high proportion of wisdom, old men are usually more productive and may be reproductive. *Do not be annoyed because of today, you are still going to face tomorrow.*

CHAPTER ELEVEN

PERSPECTIVE OF NIGERIA CONCEPT

When this old man was talking to me and explaining many issues, I quickly remembered my country, Nigeria and the said your country. Nigeria is supposed to be the Garden of Eden that was once mentioned in the scripture. "The sun that rises in the morning is a sign of hope for brighter day, crystal rain drop in the season bring fact life in abundance". He started; I feel bad concerning your predicament in this your country you called Nigeria, this is the land of blessing from God you are blessed with everything in this country especially the nature, this is where you are supposed to value Nature most, but scandalously, your misfortune invest wisely, Nigeria would have become a faultless paragon of virtues, you had succeeded in many ways dramatizing before a global audience your culture of nonchalant attitude which leads to vicissitude.

Particularly by towing foreign religion. The old man said he cannot fully discuss the historical perspective of Nigeria's political and economic development because of the complex heterogeneous nature of the country which comprises more than two hundred and fifty ethnic groups. Nigeria from time immemorial had their own traditional form of government and commerce, which readily suited and served their purpose; rules and regulations guiding conducts and human activities were exclusively cultural based. There were mythologies, customs, tradition, as well as convention all of which were package together as code of conduct. These towing foreign religious came to existence between 13th and 18th century, I mean Christianity and Islam, by that time what they brought for you is civilization and moral education, and they wanted to enlighten you on how to live comfortably in life. You all know the numbers of that denomination by that time, compare to denomination. In Nigeria now, millions of church goers and Muslims, you left your cradle to foreign religions which you don't know their origin and civilization does not allow you to rest again.

Religion has not taken over your life to the extent that you devoted, all your time for it especially in the Christian society. A lot of revivals have taken place. Pastors are many all over the country; churches have been turned to public liability company (P.L.C). Religious leaders are now teaching and advertising miracles and prosperity. Many people will leave their work in the morning, they will go to church for prayer with the aim of putting everything concerning their lives in order. As early as 6:00am in the morning, they will leave the place around 12:00pm in the afternoon, all that they have on them before will be collected from them through the saying that, you must not come before God empty handed, they will also promise them that as they give to God they are building their houses in heaven. Your people are now convinced. If they see and imagine all the atrocities being performed by the religious leaders, in this country, you have situations where pastors used his own colleague for ritual because of fame. And Muslims Alfa with the head of new born baby. In Nigeria, you have experienced religious crises especially in the northern part where many people lost their lives; you are killing yourselves because of religious whose origin you know absolutely nothing about. To say the fact, poverty is what led your people to churches and mosques. They believed that through prayer, they can overcome poverty, but they forget that poor economic conditions in the country caused poverty. Unemployment is your major problem. Poverty had veiled many personalities to the extent that they do not know their civic rights and obligations again.

In Nigeria, most people believe that politics is a dirty game because of the violence they experienced from it. Your country gained independence in 1960 and became a Republic in 1963; you have had three civilian presidents and eight military heads of state. During this period coup d'état, political violence, kidnapping and assassination did not allow you to rest. Money laundering has become the new 'national anthem'. In Nigeria, what you are practicing now is democracy, but many people "Tagged" it demonstration of craziness. You said you are one Nigeria where you have ninety-nine standing and forty-nine seating, suffering and smiling.

In the area of employment, when people want to engage themselves, some questions are posed to them such as, where is your reference letter? Who sponsored this person? Who do you know here? And to say the fact social inequality is thus an unconsciously evolved device by which societies ensure that most important positions are conscientiously filled by the most qualified person. This begins to answer the question but there are many problems it does not solve. How much of a reward is needed to motivate the right person to do the essential tasks? In Nigeria today, for example, some people make a thousand naira a day, a few make as much as ten thousand naira a day, but many make less than a thousand naira a year. Is that not too much? But remember that a central characteristic of stratification is its permanence. Those who are in favorable positions are well placed to ensure that their children get a head start.

The functional explanation of stratification, in short is only a beginning, to it must be added a power explanation, stratification exists because some persons partly by chance, have attained superior income, power and prestige, and these resources give them the necessary instruments for maintaining their position. Under conditions of rapid change of environment, the position is by no means entirely secured, as a person with few advantages, may be more vigorous in the pursuit of scarce values than those at top. The old adage "three generation from shirt sleeves to shirt sleeves" is not without some truth; yet alongside it must be part of the home truth that the best way to be successful is to embark on a step in which the ideology and the institutional pattern emphasize public advantages. Particularly education for all. In Nigeria, your leaders enjoy scholarship during their time but now scholarship is for the children of people in high social class. School fees are increased every year; it is as if they do not want the children of common man to have education. To say the fact authoritative robbery is more than armed robbery.

Nigeria as a nation comprises many ethnic groups which try to dominate the others. Nigeria is developing economically and educationally, but socially you are yet to develop, you have gotten to a certain stage in this country, that if you are not an ex-military officer, royal family and successful business man, you cannot strive for power why? To say the fact, the present government met an already corrupted society, a nation of bad international repute, high level of poverty, degraded economy and deteriorated infrastructures. In its effort to place Nigeria on a sound footing and for her to compete favorably with the outside world, a lot of economic reforms were implemented and there are still some in the pipeline. Some of these economic reforms are privatization of some government owned companies, deregulation of the downstream oil sector monetization policy for the public officers to discourage wastage, supporting agricultural sector to ensure self-sufficiency in food and raw materials. This government also succeeded in obtaining debt forgiveness up to fifty percent to African countries, although Nigerians yet to feel the impacts of these reforms.

I mentioned that **Love** is what you need to wipe away the stigma of poverty in your societies, but it seems to me that it is very difficult for love to operate in a poverty zone like Nigeria. The truth is what you need to succeed, but your people do not want it. There are many questions for you to answer. Are you practicing religion the way they do from their source? Can you say leaders are your problems? Are you free from external control? Do Nigerians operate a democratic government in the real sense of the word? Lastly, are you not still in the primitive stage of life? Where life was nasty and brutal. Where are you going from here? The old man asked, but everybody should remember that some are yet to know where they belong. Your modern societies generally should give room for the young ones to discover new things and new idea to loom.

What you done for yourself alone die with you, what you done for others and the world remains immortal. I have come, I have saved and with the help of God and the solid support, one was able to achieve quantifiable measure of success like an actor. I have played my part, now I belief that the consequences of my explanation will subsequently wipe away the stigma of poverty and alienation which like snow had veiled some personalities in the past, so also, modern people with modern problems should not base their life on religion, because "it is better to base your life on positive personality rather than religion", this will enable you to be liberated, in this case you should use the method of checks and balances on whatever is given to you in this modern society especially religion. The world indeed is a stage. Furthermore, the issue of origin and nature of people is a contemporary issue in the world. This has led to discrimination among the races, so also the aspect of religion in humanity which also brings segregation between nature and people.

The reason I am here with you is to provide up to date compendiums for you concerning those issues, which have led to conflicts among the people. Always remember this, you can never say who your best friend is because every day you seek for your daily bread, so also when the world is going to come to an end as a being. Misinformation and over-civilization has accompanying dehumanization in your modern society.

Millions of people are living in bondage through the illusion of religions, they are far away from the reality of life that is why, most people are inching the world to end abruptly which is rather impossible.

The purpose of my telling you this is to try and unite the people of the world and to live in peace as you mentioned earlier, because all that are supposed to give your life meaning had been "tagged". As **abomination**, especially nature which is yours. I hope this information will prove more interesting, useful and enjoyable for you, but what I am particular about is your freedom this is platitudes, all the censure are highly welcome. I finally woke up and

I asked myself is this a dream? *But if the wise do not support the poll, the nuisance will continue to rule.*

82